Contents

DOMESDAY
then and now

Written by Nicholas Whines
Landscapes by Peter North

BBC PUBLICATIONS

Picture Credits

AEROFILMS Richmond, Yorks. 4–5; ALFRED DUNHILL LTD *London Street Scene with Posters* by J.O. Parry *detail* (photo: John Webb) 29; ATOMIC POWER CONSTRUCTIONS LTD Trawsfynydd Atomic Power Station 42 *top*; BARNABY'S PICTURE LIBRARY toll house nr. Tavistock, Devon 27 *bottom*, North Leverton Mill, Notts. 30; BBC 6–7 *all*, Beverley, Humberside (photo: Geoff Howard) 26; NICK BIRCH Hoover Factory, Perivale 38; BRITISH LIBRARY harvesting scene MS Cott Tib BV6v 713500 13 *top*, scenes from Luttrell Psalter ADD MS 42130 13 *bottom* & 17 *both*; CAMERA PRESS M25 motorway (photo: Malcom Pendrill) 43; J. ALLAN CASH PHOTOLIBRARY Postbridge, Devon 14 *top*, Brent Park superstore 42 *bottom*; PETER CRAWLEY Newcastle upon Tyne 48; GUARDIAN NEWSPAPER Ribblehead Viaduct (photo: Denis Thorpe) 34 *top*; HATFIELD HOUSE *Fete at Bermondsey* by Hofnaegel *detail* (photo: John R. Freeman Ltd) 21; INNER LONDON EDUCATION AUTHORITY Smallwood Junior School, Wandsworth 35; A. F. KERSTING Hedingham Castle, Essex 15, Great Coxwell tithe barn, Berks. 18, Pembroke Castle, Dyfed & Amberley Church, Sussex 19, Lavenham Guildhall, Suffolk 22 *top*, Fairford Church, Glos. 23, Claremont House, Surrey 27 *top*; LAING ART GALLERY, NEWCASTLE UPON TYNE *Hiking* by James Walker Tucker (reproduced by kind permission of Tyne & Wear Museums) 37; MANCHESTER CITY ART GALLERY *Christening Sunday* by James Charles *detail* 33; NATIONAL MONUMENTS RECORD Bradford on Avon Church, Wilts. 14 *bottom*; NATIONAL PORTRAIT GALLERY *The Sharp Family* by Zoffany *detail* 25; DEREK PRATT St Ives bridge, Cambs. 22 *bottom*, Foxton Locks, Leics. 31; PUBLIC RECORD OFFICE 10 (photo: Alecto Editions Ltd), 11; JOHN D. SHARP cinema, Weston-super-Mare, Avon 39 *bottom*; THOMAS PHOTOS, OXFORD Oxford villa 34 *bottom*; TOPHAM PICTURE LIBRARY Battersea Power Station 39 *top*.

Many of the themes introduced in this book are developed in the BBC Schools Television series *Now and Then*, first transmitted on BBC2 from September 1986.

Colour landscapes by Peter North.

Tapestry illustrations on pages 8 and 9 by Alan Burton.

Sketches on pages 44, 45, 46 and 47 by Richard Gieger.

Consultant: Trevor Rowley, Assistant Director of the Department for External Studies, University of Oxford.

The author wishes to thank Bernard Cavender, the designer of this book.

This book is set in 10/12 pt Photina
Printed in England by Jolly & Barber Ltd, Rugby

Published at the request of the School Broadcasting Council for the United Kingdom by BBC Publications, a division of BBC Enterprises Limited, 35 Marylebone High Street, London W1M 4AA
First published 1986
© BBC Enterprises Limited 1986

ISBN: 0 563 21253 5

Introduction

In the year 1085 King William I ordered a great survey of all England. It was said at the time that the investigation was conducted so carefully that not a yard of ground or a single ox went unnoticed.

In 1985, 900 years later, thousands of children all over Britain carried out a new Domesday Survey. Unlike King William's commissioners who recorded their information using parchment and pen these recent investigators used detailed maps, cameras and microcomputers to record the information they collected.

The countryside through which William's commissioners rode has changed a great deal compared with the country the children explored. Where once there were muddy tracks there are now booming motorways. Some of the villages mentioned in William's survey have grown into large cities, while others have disappeared without trace. Vast areas of woodland and marsh have gone. Ancient meadows have disappeared. In King William's day the population of England was about two million, almost all of whom lived in the countryside. Today the population is around 47 million, most of whom live in towns.

Yet not everything has changed. A few churches still stand as they did in the days of King William. Mill-wheels still turn on much the same spot they occupied then. Castle mounds built by William's supporters are still visible. In fact, one thing the children who took part in the survey could not help noticing was the large number of 'left-overs' from previous ages that still exist: medieval barns; Tudor houses; eighteenth-century canals and nineteenth-century railway bridges. Even in the most modern housing estates echoes of the past can still be heard in the street names, which have been chosen as reminders of a previous age.

So to celebrate the publication of the New Domesday Survey and all the hard work so many schools put into it we have asked the artist Peter North to draw a series of landscapes showing how things have changed over the centuries. Peter's pictures show quite clearly that what we see today usually results from what has happened in the past. Most of that past has gone but enough remains to give us important clues about the lives of the people who lived before us.

The photograph on the left shows Richmond, a small market town in Yorkshire. If you look carefully you can see the castle which was built by the Normans and the church that was built some years later.

Peter North has decided to illustrate an imaginary town in order to show a wider range of features than any single town would possess. He has called his town Aldersford. It is an imaginary place but the way it develops is quite similar to the way many small towns in England grew up.

Peter's illustrations are full of detail. We hope you will enjoy examining them and comparing Aldersford with the place where you live. First of all, let's find out a little more about the great Domesday Project of 1985.

In 1985 children from schools all over the United Kingdom took part in the Domesday Project. Each school was given a block of land to investigate. In addition to finding out how land was used and what facilities were available in their area, schools also reported on the interesting and the unusual things that made their patch distinctive. The children took photographs, recorded interviews and did a great deal of research.

The Domesday Project

The information the schools gathered was fed back to the Domesday Project using their own microcomputers.

All this data collected from schools and elsewhere has now been published on two interactive video discs. Amazing as it may seem, the discs are about the size of an ordinary LP record, yet they contain a great deal more information than King William and his commissioners were able to include in their survey.

So, in the future, historians who want to know what life was like in Britain in the 1980s will be able to consult this modern electronic Domesday book.

But just as modern historians need to be able to translate and interpret the original Domesday Book, so future historians will need a special disc player and a micro to discover exactly what evidence the discs contain.

The Domesday Survey

In the year 1066 Duke William of Normandy de-feated Earl Harold at the Battle of Hastings. So William became King of England and owner of all its land. In the years which followed, William granted lands to his supporters. In return they promised to be loyal to him. In this way William imposed his control over the country he had conquered.

But what had he conquered? William knew very little about his new-won kingdom. What he did know was that there were continual disputes over who held what land. Some Norman knights, he dis-covered, had seized more land than they were en-titled to. There were complaints and quarrels. William decided to settle these matters once and for all.

The problems facing the Norman commissioners were enormous. The local English people mis-trusted them as foreigners and were unwilling to answer questions. The Norman commissioners spoke French while those they interviewed did not. Dialects differed from place to place. Words had different meanings.

Sometimes it was not clear who held a piece of land when two men both claimed it as theirs. If the matter could not be settled by a discussion a trial by combat was ordered in which the two claim-ants had to fight it out. The winner was then regarded as the rightful holder of the land.

At Christmas in the year 1085 King William met his councillors. He told them that they must conduct a great survey. He wanted to know all about the people he ruled and the land they cultivated. He wanted to establish who held what land, what the land was worth, what taxes ought to be paid and what taxes were paid.

The Council obeyed William's command. England was divided into seven circuits or areas. To each circuit were sent three of four royal commissioners to investigate every village and town. The commissioners rode on horseback. They were accompanied by several monks or scribes to write down the answers to King William's questions.

When the commissioners had completed their work, they took their findings to Winchester. Here the King's Chief Steward copied the results of the survey in Latin. He left out much of the information the commissioners had gathered. He used many abbreviations, shortening words to save space. So the Domesday Book is like a message in code.

King William never lived to make much use of his great survey of England. In 1087 he was injured while fighting in France and never recovered. In September he died. Nevertheless his survey proved very valuable to the kings who ruled after him and continues to provide remarkably detailed evidence of what England was like 900 years ago.

7 viii bord de i uirg 7 iii cot — de v ac
7 xii serui 7 xl vi burg gredd graniu xl sol.
Ibi vi molini de lxviii sol 7 i quort de vi sol
7 viii den 7 iiii quort — qui nil reddt. pasta ad pecun
uille. pru xxviii car 7 xx sol desup plus. Silua
xxx porc 7 ii arpenn uinee. Ad hoc m panent
iii bereuu 7 ibi fuer T.R.E. In totis ualentiis ualt
xxx v lib 7 do recep simil T.R.E. xl lib. hoc m
tenuit 7 iacet in dnio eccle s PETRI.

m SULESBERIE ten abb s petri p vii hid. Tra vi
car e ibi. Ad dniu pan iiii h 7 i car ibi e. Villi
hnt iiii car 7 i pbr he dm uirg 7 viii uilli
qsq i uirg 7 ii uilli de i uirg 7 v bord de i uirg
7 v cot 7 i seru. pru vi car. Pasta ad pecun uille.
In totis ualentiis ualet vi lib 7 do recep similit
T.R.E. vii lib. hoc m fuit 7 est in dnio eccle s PETRI.

m SCEPERTONE ten abb s petri p viii hid. Tra
e ad vii car. Ad dniu pan iiii h 7 dm 7 ibi est
i car uilli hnt vi car. Ibi xiii uilli qsq de i uirg
pbr xv ac 7 iii cot de vi ac 7 iii cot 7 ii serui
pru vii c. pasta ad pecun uille 7 i quort de vi
sol 7 viii den. In tot ualt vi lib 7 do recep sunt
T.R.E. vii lib. hoc m fuit e in dnio eccle s PETRI.

In HELETORNE HUNDRET

m GRENEFORDE ten abb s petri p xi hid 7 dm
Tra e vii car. Ad dniu pan v hid 7 i car ibi e
7 alia potest fieri. Villi hnt v car. Ibi i uilt he
i hid 7 i uirg 7 iiii uille qsq de dm hid 7 iiii uilli
de i hid 7 vii bord de i hid. 7 da franc i hida
7 i uirg 7 iii serui. Silua ccc porc. pasta
ad pecun uille. In totis ualent ualt vii lib 7 do
recep simil T.R.E. x lib. hoc m iacuit 7 iacet
in dnio eccle s PETRI.

m HANEWELLE ten abb s petri p viii hid se defend
Tra v car. Ad dniu pan iiii h 7 i uirg 7 i car ibi e
Villi hnt iii car. Ibi i uilt de ii hid 7 iiii uilli
de i hid 7 vi bord de iii uirg 7 iiii cot 7 ii serui
Ibi i molin de ii sol 7 ii den. pru i car. Silua
l porc. In tot ualet ualt c 7 x sol 7 do recep
simit T.R.E. vii lib. hoc m fuit 7 e in dnio s PETRI.

m COVELIE ten abb s petri p ii hid se defend
Tra e ii car. Ad dniu pan i hida 7 dm 7 ibi e i
car. Ibi ii uilli de dm h 7 i cot pru dim car.

---

pasta ad pec uille. Silua xl porc 7 molin de vi sol
7 tria uac xx sol. 7 do recep similit T.R.E. xl sol.
hanc tra tenuit 7 tenet in dnio s ptr Westmon.

In HVND DE GARE. ten Willo cameraci sub abbe
s petri ii hid 7 dm in Chingheberie. Tra ii car
In dnio i car 7 uilli i car. Ibi v uilli qsq de i uirg
7 ii cot Silua cc porc. In tra ualt xx sol 7 do recep
similit T.R.E. lx sol. hanc tra tenuit Aluuin horne
tegn regis E. in uadimonio de qda hoe s PETRI.

m HANDONE ten abb s petri p xx hid se defend
Tra xvi car. Ad dniu pan x hide 7 ibi sunt iiii
car Villi hnt viii car 7 adhuc post fieri. Ibi
pbr he i uirg 7 iii uille qsq dm h 7 vii uilli
qsq i uirg 7 xvi uilli qsq dim uirg 7 xii bord
q tenent dim hid 7 vi cot 7 i seru pru ii boii.
Silua mille porc 7 x sol. In tra ualet vii vii
lib 7 do recep similit T.R.E. xii lib. hoc m
iacuit 7 iacet in dnio eccle s PETRI.

N. TERRA SCE TRINITATIS DE MONTE ROTOM.
m HERMODESWORDE tenet abb s TRINITATIS
de rege q xxx hid se defend. Tra e xx car.
Ad dniu pan viii hide 7 ibi sunt iii car. In
franc 7 uillos sunt x car 7 vii adhuc poss ee.
Ibi qda miles he ii hid 7 ii uilli qsq i h 7 ii uille
de i h 7 xiii uilli qsq de i uirg 7 vi uilli qsq de
dim uirg 7 vi bord qsq v ac 7 vii cot 7 vi serui.
Ibi iii molini de lx sol 7 qingent anguill. de piscinis.
mille anguille. pru xx car. pasta ad pecun uille.
Silua qingent porc 7 i arpen uinee. In tra ualent
ualt xx lib 7 do recep xii lib. T.R.E. xx v lib. hoc
m tenuit com Herald 7 in hoc m fuit qda sochs ten
ii hid de hns xxx h n potuit dare l uende ext
hermodesworde T.R.E.

In SPELETORNE HVND ten Herald m de rege
i hid. Tra dim car. Ibi e un uilt q tenet ea pru
dim car. Tra ra ualt x sol 7 do recep similit T.R.E.
similit hanc tra tenuit Goldin ho comitis Heraldi
n potuit uende l dare sine ei licentia.

TERRA ECCLE DE BERCHINGES. In OSVLVESTANE HD
m TVRNE ten abbatissa de Berchinges de rege.
p v hid se defend. Tra iii car. In dnio ii hide
7 ibi e i car. Villi hnt ii car. Ibi ii uilli de dim h
7 i uills de dim uirg 7 i bord de x ac 7 ii cot
pasta ad pecun uille. Silua l porc. De herbagiu
xl den. In totu ualt l ii sol 7 do recep similit T.R.E.
c sol. hoc m iacuit 7 iacet in eccle de Berchinges.

HOLY TRINITY ABBEY, ROUEN (**1**) *holds* HERMONDESWORDE (**2**) *from the King. It answers for 30 hides.* (**3**) *Land for 20 ploughs* (**4**). *8 hides belong to the Lordship; 3 ploughs there. There are 10 ploughs between the Frenchmen* (**5**) *and the villagers; a further 7 ploughs possible* (**6**). *A man-at-arms* (**7**) *has 2 hides; 2 villagers, 1 hide each; 2 villagers with 1 hide; 14 villagers with 1 virgate* (**8**) *each; 6 villagers with ½ virgate each, 6 smallholders* (**9**), *5 acres each; 7 cottagers* (**10**); *6 slaves* (**11**); *3 mills at 60 shillings, and 500 eels* (**12**); *from the fishponds 1000 eels; meadow for 20 ploughs; pasture for the village livestock* (**13**); *woodland, 500 pigs* (**14**); *1 arpent of vines* (**15**). *Total value* (**16**) *£20; when acquired £12; in the time of King Edward £25.*

Earl Harold held this manor (**17**). *In this manor there was a Freeman* (**18**) *who held 2 of those 30 hides; in the time of King Edward he could not grant or sell this land outside Hermondesworde.*

Here is the Domesday entry for the village of Harmondsworth in Middlesex. It stands just to the west of London Airport.

It must have been much quieter in 1085, at the time of the survey, than it is today.

Here are some notes to help you understand what the entry for Harmondsworth means.

(**1**)   The manor of Harmondsworth was granted to a French monastery in Rouen.

(**2**)   Notice the place names are slightly different.

(**3**)   A hide was an amount of land – perhaps 120 acres. No one is absolutely sure how much. It is unlikely if it was ever carefully measured out.

(**4**)   This is another way of describing an area of land: one requiring 20 teams of oxen to plough it.

(**5**)   This probably refers to settlers from France who have arrived since the Conquest.

(**6**)   This suggests that not all the land was cultivated.

(**7**)   This is a man who had to give military service for his land.

(**8**)   A virgate was a quarter of a hide.

(**9**)   Smallholders were middle class peasants.

(**10**)   A cottager was someone who owned a house but little or no land.

(**11**)   A slave was someone who had to work for another person and who was not free to do anything without permission.

(**12**)   Rent for the water-mill was paid for in money and eels!

(**13**)   Common land on which everybody in the village could graze their animals.

(**14**)   This gives an idea of how much woodland there was – enough for 500 pigs to find food (acorns) in.

(**15**)   An arpent was an acre. The vines grew grapes for wine-making.

(**16**)   The total income of the manor is given for three dates.

(**17**)   This is Earl Harold who was killed at the Battle of Hastings.

(**18**)   A Freeman was an independent peasant who was of higher class than the other villagers. But he wasn't free to sell his land to anybody outside the manor.

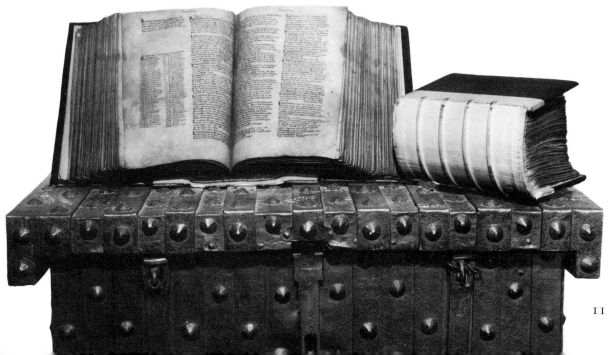

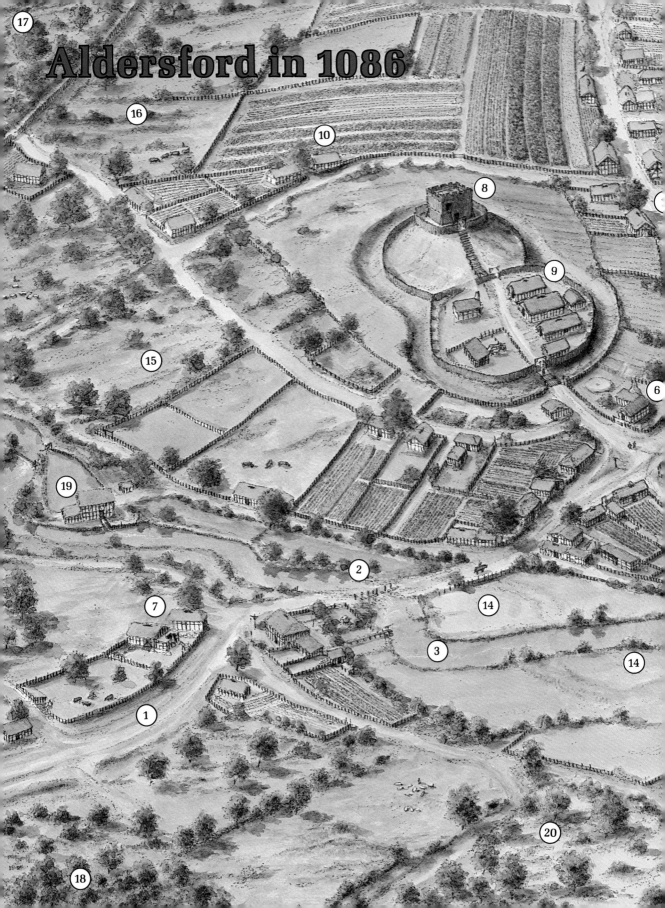

Aldersford in 1086

Making hay.

A water-mill.

T his is the village of Aldersford as it might have been in the year 1086. It is an imaginary place but not very different from many English villages of the time. We are looking north west.

At the time of the Norman Conquest England was already a rich agricultural country. Most of the forests which once spread across the country had been cleared and the land now farmed. It was a country well worth conquering.

Why did a village grow up at this particular spot? The answer is that here a busy path, called the Wealdway (1), drops down to the valley bottom to *ford* (2) the River Alder (3). The water is shallow and it provides a good place to cross.

The village of Aldersford lies to the south of the river on a low hill. If the river floods, the village stays dry.

A ford is a good place for a settlement to develop so people have

This is a clapper bridge at Postbridge in Devon. It is one of the simplest forms of stone bridge you can find.

almost certainly lived here in Roman times and even earlier.

The village takes it name from a Saxon chief called Aldred, who lived here in the sixth century. He also gave his name to the river.

The only stone building in the village is the church (4). It is about 100 years old and replaced a wooden church that was destroyed by fire. Compared with churches we know today, it is very small. It is little more than one room. Like all the other village buildings it has a *thatched* roof. The villagers' houses are very simple wooden-framed buildings. The low walls are made by weaving together strips of wood (*wattle*) and covering them with a mixture of clay, straw and animal manure (*daub*). Inside these houses *rushes* are used to cover the bare earth.

Some of the other buildings in the village you can see are the granary (5) where corn was stored, a bakehouse (6) and a smithy (7).

At the Battle of Hastings the *thegn* who held the village was killed. Shortly after the battle, King William gave the land to the north of the river to one of his Norman supporters. This man is now strengthening his position by building a castle (8) close to the village. He has constructed a mound of earth and rock called a *motte*. On top of this he has built a wooden tower. In a few years' time he will begin building a stone *keep*. To one side of the motte lies the *bailey* where the Norman knight has constructed his hall (9). Surrounding the hall and the bailey is a ditch and strong wooden fence. Here he lives with his family and a small group of armed men.

From his castle the Norman knight controls both the village and the river crossing. If the villagers rebel against his authority he can retreat to the safety of his castle.

The villagers do not rebel but accept their new overlord. He in turn requires the villagers to farm part of the land.

In return for their land the villagers have to give a certain

This is one of the oldest churches in the country – St Lawrence, Bradford-on-Avon. It was built around the year 700.

amount of the food they produce to their lord and help him for a number of days every year with the work on his land, which is called the *demesne* or home farm (10).

The farmland is divided into three large fields. Within these fields the villagers are allowed to cultivate strips. On some strips they grow cereal crops such as wheat, barley or oats (11). On others they grow peas and beans (12). Some of the land is left unplanted or *fallow* to give the soil a chance to rest (13).

Down by the river are the *water meadows* (14). Here grass is grown as a crop. In the summer this will be cut and used to feed the animals in winter and provide bedding for them. *Pasture* is land used for grazing animals (15).

The village has some common land where all the villagers are allowed to graze their animals (16).

The Lord of the Manor has retained much of the forest that lies to the east of his castle for himself (17). Later he will turn this into a deer park where he and his followers can hunt. Fences and ditches will be built to keep the deer in and the villagers out.

In other areas of woodland the villagers are allowed to graze their pigs on the acorns and pick up firewood (18).

On the river is a water-mill (19). Here the miller grinds the villagers' corn into flour. He keeps a bit back for himself as payment. Sometimes he keeps too much. The miller pays rent to the Lord of the Manor.

The Norman knight would like to extend his control to the land on the other side of the river (20). However, King William has already decided to keep the land for himself. In 100 years' time it will be given to a group of monks who wish to build a new monastery.

This is the keep at Hedingham Castle in Essex. It was built in 1141.

Aldersford in 1286

Ploughing with a team of oxen.

Using hurdles to make a sheepfold.

Two hundred years have passed since we last saw the village of Aldersford. Great changes have taken place. Before you read any further, compare this view with that on pages 12 and 13.

The River Alder still follows much the same course. So does the road we call the Wealdway.

The ancestors of the Norman knight who fought with King William have been very successful. They have grown enormously rich. Much of their money has been spent improving their castle. First of all the original motte was flattened and a square keep (1) was built with rooms for the Lord and his family, his soldiers and servants.

Years later a curtain wall was built surrounding the bailey. In places it is 20 metres high.

Later still towers have been added and a strong gateway (2). In 1286 England is fairly peaceful and prosperous. The Lord doesn't really need such a fortified home. The truth is that this castle has been built to impress everybody and let everybody know that it is the home of an important man.

Where has all the money come from? In the past the family made their money out of the Crusades and by supporting the King. Today, however, it is sheep which are making them wealthy.

The Wealdway has become a drovers' road along which sheep are taken to market. Lines of pack horses laden with valuable wool frequently pass by.

The Lord's masons have built a strong pack-bridge (3) across the River Alder and travellers are charged a *toll* for using it.

With all this traffic on the road the Lord has obtained a *licence* from the King to hold a weekly market (4). The market is very successful

and the village of Aldersford grows rapidly as more and more crafts-men and traders move in. Simple inns (5) are built to provide travellers with food and lodging. Larger houses are built for merchants who have come to live in Aldersford (6). By 1286 there are two general markets and one animal market each week. A market house is built in the centre of the market place and the market is run from this building (7).

In 1300 the king grants Aldersford a Royal Charter making the place a borough. The leading merchants are known as burgesses and form Aldersford's governing body. Aldersford is no longer a village but a town.

With all this activity it is not surprising that a wharf area has developed on the river bank so that heavier goods can be brought in by water (8), including the stone

for building the castle and re-building the church.

The church is very important in the lives of the people. Most people attend the services. The church porch is used to conduct marriages and for business contracts to be signed. The area round the church is an important social centre. On holidays it is used for feasts and merry-making.

The priest is appointed by the Lord. Notice his tithe barn (9). His parishioners have to give him one tenth (tithe) of their produce to maintain him and his church.

The little Saxon church has changed. Several times in the last 200 years the people of Aldersford have worked together to enlarge and beautify their church. First a solid Norman tower was built and later the church was re-roofed. But the parish church is dwarfed by the great monastery church being built

The tithe barn at Great Coxwell in Berkshire.

Pembroke Castle was completed about 1250.

on the south side of the river (10).

To the south of the river the monks and the laybrothers who help them have been as busy as the townsfolk of Aldersford

The monks spend a great deal of time in their church praying. But they have also organised a huge building programme. In addition to the church itself you can see the cloisters, the chapter house, the dining room, the wash rooms, the bedrooms, the hospital, the tithe barn (11) and the abbot's house (12).

The wealth of the monks comes from the sheep they raise. The monks offer shelter for the night to travellers. They have built a house for this purpose by the road (14).

The monks are also good engineers. They have brought water into their buildings to operate a mill and to fill their fishponds (13) and for washing and sanitation. They have also drained much marshy land which can now be used for farming.

This is the church of St Michael at Amberley in Sussex. Much of it was rebuilt during the thirteenth century.

Aldersford in 1586

A wedding feast.

We have taken another huge leap through the history of our imaginary town. Three hundred years have gone by. Plague and war have both visited the town. There have been dark days. Now Aldersford is growing once again. Elizabeth I is Queen of England and Aldersford prospers.

Aldersford still has its sheep. But the town no longer exports raw wool. Instead woven cloth is sent to the Continent to be made up into clothes. A group of French families have recently settled in Aldersford. They had to leave their own country because of religious persecution. They have been teaching the Aldersford weavers a number of new techniques for improving the quality of their cloth.

The weavers' houses are quite distinctive (1). They have large windows to let in plenty of light. At this time people work at home

This is the Guildhall in Lavenham in Suffolk. It was built in the fifteenth century.

using hand looms. Factories are a long way in the future.

Now let's look at the monastery. What do you notice? Some of the buildings have lost their roofs. Others are partly demolished. What has happened to the monks? The answer is this: they have gone. Fifty years ago King Henry VIII forced most of the monasteries to close down. He then sold off the monastery lands to his supporters.

A rich merchant from Aldersford has bought up some of the land and has rebuilt the abbot's house for himself and his family (2). The monastery guest house is now used as an inn (3).

Now let's look at the castle. Today massive castles like this are no longer needed in peaceful Aldersford. Over the last 300 years it has changed hands many times. Sometimes the family died out and

there was no one to inherit it. Sometimes the owner quarrelled with the King and the castle was taken away from him. In 1586, however, few people want to live in a cold, draughty castle.

The castle now belongs to Queen Elizabeth. She has let it to her representative in this area, the *County Sheriff*. He has built himself a house within the bailey and laid out a neat garden (4). However the old

Fairford Church in Gloucestershire, built towards the end of the fifteenth century.

keep and walls are in a poor state. People are continually stealing the stones to repair their houses and the local roads.

Sometimes Queen Elizabeth comes to the forest to hunt. As a result the Sheriff has built a hunting lodge (5). The Queen is very impressed.

In Aldersford people are building themselves substantial timber-framed houses. Sometimes these are *infilled* with bricks or *lathe and plaster*. Many of the new houses have brick chimneys. Tiles have replaced thatch as the most fashionable roofing material. Notice that the upper *storeys* of the houses project over the lower storey. This increases the amount of room in a house without requiring more land. This feature is known as a *jetty*.

Other jettied buildings can also be seen. The guildhall (6) is an im-pressive building where the mayor lives and where the town council holds its meetings. Here prices are fixed, by-laws agreed, ale-tasters appointed, weights and measures checked and the quality of Alders-ford's cloth examined.

A grammar school has been es-tablished to educate the children of Aldersford's townsfolk (7). At the grammar school the boys and girls work very hard at their lessons. Time is also allowed for such activities as archery, hawking and learning a musical instrument, perhaps the lute or the virginal.

The school was paid for by a rich merchant who had made a great deal of money out of the wool trade. He also paid for a row of almshouses to accommodate elderly people who deserved a comfortable home (8).

All the town contributed towards the construction of a fine new stone bridge crossing the River Alder (9). The old one was swept away in the great flood of 1508. The monastery gave money for a small chapel to be built on their side of the bridge. Here travellers could pray for a safe journey. The bridge is wide enough for two wagons to pass and there are refuges for pedestrians above each *pier*.

The church is looking finer than ever. Much of it has been rebuilt. The nave has been greatly en-larged and a new tower has been added. Notice that there is now a lych gate at the entrance to the churchyard (10). This provides shelter for the bodies of the dead on their way to burial.

The market square is never big enough. Several times it has been enlarged. At the market hall (11) taxes and tolls are collected and arguments between buyers and sellers sorted out.

There are now an increasing number of shops. Some of these are little more than workshops with a window giving onto the street. But increasingly there are shops as we know them, where goods are brought to be sold. Most buying and selling, however, still takes place in the market which is now held every day.

In the countryside there is far less prosperity. While the big land-owners with their huge flocks of sheep grow richer and richer, smallholders find life hard. Many of them have been *evicted* and their land turned over to sheep.

Large numbers of landless beggars roam the countryside. The town council is continually discussing what to do with the increasing number of families who, having lost their land, have lost their livelihood.

Left This is the bridge across the Great Ouse at St Ives in Cambridgeshire. It was built in 1414.

Aldersford in 1786

THE DOMESDAY PROJECT

In 1085 William the Conqueror ordered the Domesday book to be written so that he could learn all he needed about the land and the people of Britain.

900 years later the BBC decided to commemorate William's book with another survey. They called it the Domesday project and it has turned out very differently from William's original book. For a start it is electronic. This means you can call up any one of tens of thousands of photographs at the press of a button; there are maps to zoom round; film clips to watch and hundreds of thousands of pages of writing and facts to explore.

The Domesday Project is like an enormous electronic album showing life in the United Kingdom today.

People from all over the United Kingdom have contributed to the modern Domesday survey and by using up-to-the-minute technology the BBC has managed to store all the information which has been collected on just two interactive laser videodiscs. A videodisc is the size of an LP record.

To play an interactive videodisc you need a special videodisc player which is controlled by a microcomputer. You use the microcomputer to ask for any of the information on the disc and in seconds your request is displayed on the television screen.

COMMUNITY DISC

The first Domesday disc is called the Community Disc. It is the story of life in the United Kingdom in the 1980s as described and photographed by people who really know their own area well.

How the Community Disc was made

The first thing the BBC did was to divide the country into 23,000 blocks each measuring four kilometres across and three kilometres up. It then invited every school in the country to take part in a national survey. In some areas schools took whole blocks and in other areas they shared a block. The BBC realised that schools could use their own computers to record their work. This was extremely important because it meant that the surveys could be fed immediately into the large BBC computer and so save an incredible amount of time typing all the information in again by hand.

School research teams conducted their surveys throughout 1985. They interviewed local VIPs and knowledgeable residents, found out what was important or worrying in their block, took photographs and then prepared their reports and recorded them using a microcomputer. At the end of the summer, floppy discs, cassettes and photographs started arriving back at the Domesday Project office by the sackful. All the floppy discs and cassettes were sent to Loughborough University where they were carefully checked. It took six people six months to read all the text for the community disc and they were not even correcting

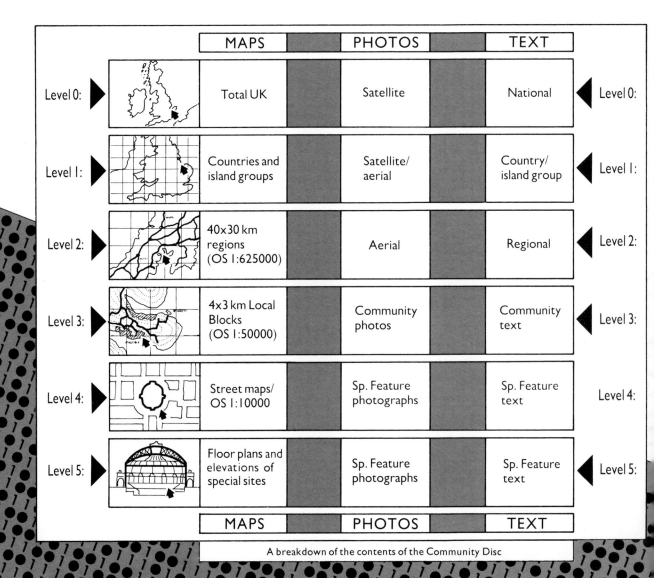

	MAPS		PHOTOS		TEXT	
Level 0:	Total UK		Satellite		National	Level 0:
Level 1:	Countries and island groups		Satellite/aerial		Country/island group	Level 1:
Level 2:	40x30 km regions (OS 1:625000)		Aerial		Regional	Level 2:
Level 3:	4x3 km Local Blocks (OS 1:50000)		Community photos		Community text	Level 3:
Level 4:	Street maps/OS 1:10000		Sp. Feature photographs		Sp. Feature text	Level 4:
Level 5:	Floor plans and elevations of special sites		Sp. Feature photographs		Sp. Feature text	Level 5:
	MAPS		PHOTOS		TEXT	

A breakdown of the contents of the Community Disc

spelling mistakes! The information was then returned to the Domesday office where it was fed into the main-frame computer. The photographs were sent to the Open University at Milton Keynes and copied onto a videotape using a special camera. Finally, with the text, photographs, and the index of keywords all prepared, two tapes – one containing pictures, the other all the written material – were sent to the Philips Electronics factory in Blackburn and 'pressed', as the process is called, on to the Domesday Community Disc.

What makes up the Community Disc

On the Community Disc there are thousands of maps. To begin with there is a map of the whole of the United Kingdom and at this level there is a satellite photograph and a general written description. The next level down divides the United Kingdom into its countries and island groups. The level below this takes you to a county sized map and for this there are matching aerial photographs. Then down again there are the 4 × 3 km blocks of the country surveyed by schools and community groups. But it does not stop there – for the seventy largest towns and cities there are street plans and in some special areas there are even floor plans of buildings.

How to use the Community Disc

Imagine you have loaded the Community Disc into the videodisc player and you want to zoom through the maps on the disc to the town where you will be spending your holiday. You start with a map of the whole of the United Kingdom – first use the tracker ball (like a joystick) to move a pointer on the screen to the part of the county you are going to and press the button – immediately the next level of map appears. Move the pointer again and press. This time you may see the town marked and you could call up an aerial photograph to see what it looks like from a distance. Then move the pointer to the town itself and press. Now the 4 × 3 km map is displayed and you can call up the photos and descriptions written by the people who live there. You may get, for example, some good tips on what to do on your holiday. Of course if you have no idea where in the United Kingdom your holiday town is situated you can type in the place name and the right map will come up on the screen. Another way to use the disc is to ask it about something that interests you; ice skating, fishing, whatever . . . the micro will ask the disc to find everything which has been written about that subject on the Community Disc and you can select the ones you want to look at. It can find pictures in the same way too. Another thing the Community Disc can do is measure distances and areas. Have you ever wondered how far you walk to school or cycle in a week? Again, just use the pointer to draw the route you want to measure on the map, whether it's a straight line or a crazy route and the distance will be displayed at the top of the screen.

You do not have to worry about getting lost on the disc because there are lots of 'help' sections explaining everything. These consist of moving pictures and sound and will show examples of all the ways you can use the disc.

NATIONAL DISC

The second Domesday disc, the National Disc, takes an official view of the United Kingdom in the 1980s. Like the Community Disc there are many thousands of photographs and written pages – this time selected from newspapers, magazines and journals. However, the National Disc also contains film clips and statistics by the million, taken from government surveys such as the population census. It also includes the counts and land cover work completed by schools.

How to use the National Disc

The National Disc is very carefully indexed and cross-referenced, so all you have to do is type in what you want to know about and the Domesday system will display on the screen a list of everything it has got on the subject. Take 'butterflies', for example – there might be a set of photographs showing all sorts of butterflies found in the UK which you could flick through. You could see if a particular butterfly is common where you live by asking the system to find a map of the region and then to overlay a distribution pattern in colour on top of it. You could compare this distribution map with another one, say of the pied flycatcher, or find out whether another part of the country has more or fewer butterflies or pied flycatchers. If your area has no pied flycatchers at all you could see if an article had been written about the kind of habitats they need in order to thrive.

As well as wildlife and environmental information the national disc has detailed coverage of the economy, society and culture of the United Kingdom in the 1980s.

If you are the nosey or investigative type you might like to try another feature of the National Disc, a 'surrogate journey'. This could be for example a visit to somebody's stone cottage, a five-bedroomed house or a farm. You start with the outside of a house, and then use the tracker ball and pointer to move and look in any direction you please – left, right, forward, to the front door, inside, up the stairs, inside the wardrobe, in fact wherever you want.

For the National Disc, just as for the Community Disc, you choose where to go and what you want to know about and the system will show you what is there. And, of course, if you run into problems there is always the 'help' button to put you on the right track.

The Domesday Discs will be available in November 1986.

If you would like any more information on the Project please contact:

Information Officer, BBC Domesday Project,
54–58 Uxbridge Road,
London, W5 2ST.

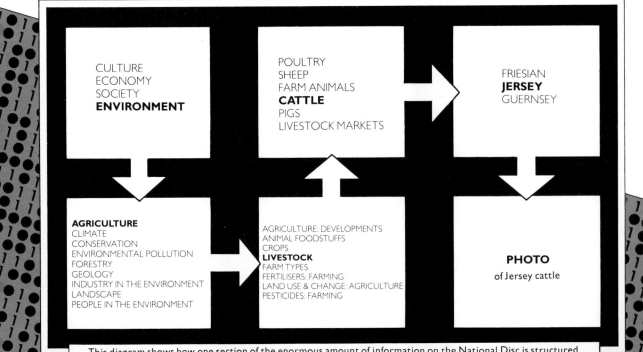

CULTURE
ECONOMY
SOCIETY
ENVIRONMENT

POULTRY
SHEEP
FARM ANIMALS
CATTLE
PIGS
LIVESTOCK MARKETS

FRIESIAN
JERSEY
GUERNSEY

AGRICULTURE
CLIMATE
CONSERVATION
ENVIRONMENTAL POLLUTION
FORESTRY
GEOLOGY
INDUSTRY IN THE ENVIRONMENT
LANDSCAPE
PEOPLE IN THE ENVIRONMENT

AGRICULTURE: DEVELOPMENTS
ANIMAL FOODSTUFFS
CROPS
LIVESTOCK
FARM TYPES
FERTILISERS: FARMING
LAND USE & CHANGE: AGRICULTURE
PESTICIDES: FARMING

PHOTO
of Jersey cattle

This diagram shows how one section of the enormous amount of information on the National Disc is structured

Wealthy townsfolk enjoying a musical outing.

Another 200 years have slipped by since we last visited Aldersford. The Stuart kings have come and gone. Now King George III sits on the throne. Times have been good and bad but on the whole Aldersford remains prosperous. It is a pleasant place to live. Never a year goes by without an old building being pulled down or a new one put up. Sometimes a building is modified an extra storey is added; a new wing is built.

Fire has always been a problem. Wooden houses roofed with thatch and built close together burn easily. Just to the north-west of the town, beyond the church, an old section of the town was completely destroyed earlier in the century. These houses have been replaced with brick-built terraces (1). No jetties are allowed. There is a good

25

space between each row of houses. Compared with the jumble of medieval and Tudor buildings, where every house is a different shape, these Georgian houses are very orderly. Bricks and glass are now much more plentiful and good use is made of them. The bricks are made locally.

In some cases the new Georgian houses are not as new as they look. Rather than build a completely new building, the builders have surrounded a timber framed house with brick walls. As a result of this, houses are sometimes much older than they look on the outside (2).

The castle is now a ruin although the keep, the gatehouse and sections of the wall still survive. Space is becoming quite a problem in Aldersford. Houses have been built in the bailey. The area surrounding the church has changed. In the last century it became the fashion for gravestones

to be placed over people's graves. Some of these are already over 100 years old. These old stones are full of interesting information about the people who lived here in the past. The churchyard is no longer the social centre it used to be. Feasts and fetes are held elsewhere.

To the south of the church the wharf area continues to be busy (4). Large quantities of coal are now delivered by barge and people burn coal on their fires. Wood is in short supply. The boatmen are always complaining to the town council that the river is *silting up*. Unless something is done it will soon be impossible for boats to reach as far upstream as Aldersford.

The people of Aldersford still weave for their living. But now they have specialised as competition from other areas gets stronger. Aldersford is becoming famous for its blankets. Many a

great man is kept warm at night by a blanket woven in Aldersford.

Big changes are taking place in the countryside. There are fewer sheep than there used to be. More land is used for growing crops and raising cattle. The owner of Abbey Farm has been buying up the land of smaller farmers as fast as he can. The old way of farming in strips is disappearing.

Efficient farmers want to *enclose* their property (5). They want to put hedges round their land, to dig drainage ditches and breed better animals. The smaller farmers don't usually want to sell but they have little choice. Worse still, the remaining common land is divided up between all the landowners. For most people their share is not enough to keep an animal on. As a result many smallholders are now forced to work for a wage as farm labourers.

For hundreds of years people have been complaining about the state of the road leading to Aldersford. In summer rock-hard ruts cause wagons to overturn or axles to break. In winter the road is so muddy that wagons stick fast. Now a group of landowners and businessman have formed a *turnpike trust*. They have taken over a stretch of road and put it in good order. They have put gates across the road (6) and charge a toll for everybody who uses the road. Can you see the toll house where the toll-keeper lives?

The toll-keeper has to keep wide awake to open the gates for travellers. The turnpike has greatly increased the trade at the Drovers Inn (7). New stables have been built as well as more accommodation for travellers.

The increased traffic has damaged the bridge which is showing

Terraced houses in Beverley in Yorkshire.

This is Claremont House in Surrey. It was built between 1768 and 1772.

signs of old age. The chapel is now used as the town gaol.

Across the fields from the turnpike is a brand new tower mill (8). This is a great improvement on the old post mill because only the top of the mill and sails moved to face the wind.

Aldersford's biggest landowner has recently moved from the old Tudor house by the river (9) to a fine modern house (10) called Aldersford Park. He demolished Queen Elizabeth's hunting lodge to make room for his new building. The style looks a bit like a temple from ancient Greece but is considered the height of fashion. The grounds of the parkland have been landscaped to make them more beautiful. An artificial lake has been dug and a fine avenue of elms planted leading up to the house.

This is a little toll house on the Tavistock to Launceston Road in Devon.

Aldersford in 1836

Putting up a poster.

This is Aldersford in the year 1836, one hundred and fifty years ago. In a year's time Queen Victoria will begin her long reign. We have moved in a little to take a closer look at Aldersford. If you look carefully you will see all sorts of small changes.

The big change is the arrival of the canal (1) which was completed in the year 1800. It forms a spur from the main canal network which has been developing over the past thirty years. The company responsible for building the canal ran out of money after they got to Aldersford, so the canal never went any further.

For nearly a year Aldersford was invaded by the *navvies*, the inland navigators, who did the hard work of digging out the canals. They did all this work using little more than wheelbarrows and shovels. The navvies were famous for their drinking and their fighting, and they terrified the townsfolk. The lock-up on the bridge was not strong enough to hold the worst offenders and so a new prison was built. By the time it was complete the canal was finished and the navvies had moved on elsewhere.

The people of Aldersford have always known how much easier it is to transport goods by water than by road. A horse-drawn barge can carry many times the amount of coal compared with a cart and four horses. As a result of the canal the price of coal has come down.

In order to enter Aldersford Dock the barges have to pass through two locks. Close to the locks you can see the lock-keeper's cottage. It is his job to operate the gates and *sluices*. The barges are pulled by horses along the tow path. Specially designed bridges have been created so the horse can cross over to the opposite bank (2). Next to the cottage are several warehouses where goods could be stored, including large numbers of Aldersford blankets. There is also an alehouse for the thirsty bargemen.

There are a great many alehouses and beershops in Aldersford. There is also a new brewery making Aldersford Ale (3). Not everybody drinks, however. The congregation of the new Methodist chapel disapprove of alchohol (4). They have wanted to build their own place of worship for a long time and now they have. They do not like going to the old church. They think the services are dull and the vicar spends too much time out hunting with his rich friends.

For some years it has been thought that plain stone or brick is ugly. In 1836 fashionable buildings are *stuccoed*, in other words covered over with a layer of plaster. The fashion will not last very much longer. Stucco looks very nice when it is new or freshly painted but it begins to look shabby very quickly.

The old bridge was getting so expensive to repair that it was decided to pull it down and start again. Aldersford now has a new bridge (5). The spans of the new bridge are much wider than those of the old one and it is large enough to take all the increased traffic pouring into the town from the turnpike.

The Drover's Inn has never done such good business (6). The landlord has become a rich man and employs a large number of people looking after travellers and their horses. Not far from the Inn is a wheelwright's shop where trade is also very good. In fact so many people want to order new vehicles that there are just not enough skilled men to make them.

The manufacture of blankets still continues in Aldersford. As yet there are no factories or power-driven looms, only the water-driven fulling mill. Most of the work is still done by people from their homes.

Unfortunately there isn't enough work to go round any more and some weavers and their families are desperately poor. Weavers are not the only people going through difficult times. People are drifting

North Leverton Mill in Nottinghamshire was built in 1813.

into Aldersford from the surrounding countryside in the hope of finding work. Some are lucky. Others are not. Those who have absolutely nothing are forced to go to the workhouse (7).

This building has only just been built. It is cold and uncomfortable. The food is poor. People who go there are forced to work in the yard at the back, breaking bones. Once in the workhouse you are not allowed out. In fact it is more like a prison than anything else. Everything is done to make sure that people only go there for help if they have no other choice but to starve. Indeed some people would rather starve than go to the workhouse.

While some people in Aldersford live well in fine new houses with plenty of servants to wait on them, others do not. They live in overcrowded rooms. The old drainage ditches which feed waste into the river can no longer cope. They are foul and evil-smelling. Only the richer homes can afford piped water. Most people have to rely on a few wells and pumps (8). Sometimes the water gets polluted and there are cases of cholera and typhoid fever. However, people still do not realise that dirt and disease go together.

If you were to visit Aldersford in 1836 you would see great contrasts of wealth and poverty existing side by side.

Foxton Locks on the Grand Union Canal were built between 1810 and 1812. It took 70 minutes for barges to pass through.

31

Aldersford in 1886

Outside the church.

The year is 1886. Queen Victoria has been on the throne for nearly fifty years. She rules over one of the largest empires the world has ever seen. The great wonder of her reign has been the railway (1). It has transformed the town of Aldersford.

Not everybody wanted it. Many people thought that it was noisy, dirty, dangerous and ugly. But in Victorian England a town without a railway was a town of declining fortune. So in 1850 the railway came to Aldersford. Railway tracks have to be more or less level so a *viaduct* had to be built to carry the railway over the existing road bridge. A sturdy station was built on the eastern side of the town (2). A few years later the Railway Hotel was constructed nearby (3).

Underneath the arches of the viaduct many small industries thrive: coach-builders, wheel-

Ribblehead viaduct in Yorkshire.

wrights, a saw mill and a coal yard. Children no longer swim in the River Alder. The water is far too *polluted*.

Many old buildings had to be knocked down to make way for the railway. Not far away a new school building has been constructed (**4**). This is an elementary school for children up to the age of ten. The law now says that all children must attend. The windows are designed to be too high for the pupils to look out of them.

The children who attend the school live in houses built in many different periods. Some live in the newly built rows of terraced housing. Aldersford is growing in size and there is a problem providing enough homes for everyone. Most of these new terraces have two rooms downstairs and two rooms upstairs, a small yard and an outside lavatory (**5**).

A large detached, Victorian house in Oxford.

A Board school in South London.

For those with more money to spend, such as clerks and shop managers, there are streets of semi-detached villas. These have an extra room for a live-in maid. They have small gardens front and back.

And for those doing well in business or the professions, large detached houses are being built on the outskirts of the town (6). These houses stand in their own grounds. They have their own carriage drive. The owners of houses like these employ plenty of servants to look after them.

Several of the gentlemen who have recently purchased these new houses are town councillors. The town council holds its meetings in the brand new town hall (7). The mayor believes that a town which is proud of itself needs a town hall to be proud of. Some people think the new building is too large and rather ugly. One project the council

is particularly proud of is the new public baths (8). This is important as few people have bathrooms in their own houses. The council have also provided the town with much needed sewers. As a result the town smells a good deal better than it did in the past – except near the gasworks (9). Some streets now have gas lighting and gas is piped into the newer homes. There is now a hospital (10) for those who fall sick.

Alongside all these improvements some people are now taking a much greater interest in the history of Aldersford. Steps have been taken to preserve the castle ruins and the monastery ruins from further decay. The monastery tithe barn has been re-roofed and is still in use (11).

Much restoration work has taken place in the church (12). The spire that was added in the eight-

eenth century has been removed. Much of the tower has been re-built and strengthened to support the weight of the bells. Unfortunately, in restoring the church a lot of what was old and interesting has been destroyed. Some people miss the old pews with their strange carvings. Somehow the church has lost the comfortable, homely feeling it once had.

The coming of the railways has had a dramatic effect on the coaching inn near the bridge (13). A journey by coach which takes all day can now be made in a hour or two on the train. Still, although the stage coaches no longer run there is still plenty of traffic on the road and the Drovers Inn manages to do good business. So does the blacksmith, as all the traffic is horse-drawn (14).

Aldersford in 1936

Hikers in the countryside.

This has been a dramatic year in British history. At home King Edward VIII has *abdicated*. He has given up his throne in order to marry the woman he loves. The new King is George VI, Edward's younger brother and the father of our present Queen. Abroad the activities of the German leader, Adolf Hitler worry the people of Aldersford. They wonder if there will be another war with Germany as there was between 1914 and 1918.

Across the market place stands the war memorial (1). It is a sad reminder of all the men from Aldersford who died during that war.

Radio now brings news of the world directly into people's homes. Although television has already been invented you won't see a single television aerial. No one in Aldersford has yet bought a set. Many houses now have electricity and a new shop has opened in Aldersford selling electrical goods. A small factory has been set up recently making vacuum cleaners.

Another new invention is the telephone. Many houses have already been 'connected up'. People who can't afford a telephone of their own can use the kiosks in the market place (2). The only trouble with the telephone is the jumble of poles and wires everywhere.

During the war Aldersford Park was taken over as a *convalescent* home where soldiers who had been injured could be nursed back to health again (3). When the war was over the old owners did not return. Houses this size are now just too big to run. The grounds are very overgrown and the house needs lots of repairs.

The old windmill is also in ruins (4). For the first time since the time of the Normans there is no mill turning in Aldersford. Flour is milled elsewhere in large factories.

Once upon a time the town produced almost everything it needed itself. In the twentieth century almost everything has to be bought in from outside.

More of these goods are now arriving by road than ever before. Even though the railway is still going strong, the age of the motor car has now reached Aldersford. Before the war few people were rich enough to run a motor car. Now many more people can afford them. As well as cars, motor buses have changed the lives of country folk. People who rarely travelled outside their own village can now come into Aldersford on market day. In fact the traffic on market day is getting worse and worse. The council complains that the more parking places they provide the more vehicles seem to arrive.

Aldersford has more to offer the visitor now. In addition to the markets and shops, there is now a fine new cinema showing a differ-

ent film every week (5). And next to the public baths there is a smart new open-air swimming pool (6).

You might think that the blacksmith will have gone out of business. In fact there are still plenty of horse-drawn carts about. But the blacksmith is moving with the times. He has set up a petrol station (7) next door to the forge and he is learning how to repair cars that have gone wrong.

Travellers still like to stay at the Drovers Inn, but now of course they arrive by car. The manager of the inn has decided to pull down his old stables and build more accommodation for his customers and a car park.

People with cars are able to live much further from the town centre than used to be the case. As a result there are plenty of people wanting to buy the new semi-detached houses going up near the old windmill (8). These houses are smaller than the Victorian semis

Battersea Power Station came into operation in 1932.

but lighter and brighter. They have bathrooms and lavatories, electricity, gas and main drainage. Best of all they are in the country away from all the noise and smell of the town.

But the farmers are worried. As more and more land disappears under houses they wonder where it will all end. Once upon a time the majority of people in this area worked on the land growing crops and raising animals. In 1936 the number of people involved in agriculture is shrinking. New machines like tractors can get far more work done than gangs of men and horses.

Left A new factory for a new age – the Hoover factory in West London.

In the 1930s the cinema was enormously popular.

Aldersford Today

This is what has happened to our imaginary town of Aldersford 900 years after King William's commissioners rode through the ford on their way to somewhere more important. This is the town the local children would have surveyed if they had taken part in the Domesday Project. If you look carefully you will see features that are similar to the place where you live. You will also see all the 'left-overs' from past ages that go to make up a modern town.

Let's examine what has happened in the last fifty years. We could start with the railway. As you can see, it has gone. In 1960 the line was closed as it was losing too much money. The viaduct was then demolished and much of the old industrial area of the town by the side of the river was re-developed.

Part of the railway line extending south east has become a nature trail (1). The station buildings have been converted into a builder's yard (2).

The canal is still there. At one time it was going to be filled in but a group of enthusiasts have been hard at work restoring the lock gates and a small museum has opened in an old warehouse (3).

In 1986 Aldersford's new industry is tourism. Each year visitors arrive from all over the world to see the remains of the past that survive here.

By 1970 traffic conditions had become quite chaotic. Everybody was very relieved when a by-pass was constructed (4) passing the town to the east. The only person to suffer was the owner of Aldersford Garage, who lost his passing trade. The new filling stations do good business (5).

Nuclear power station

Right The new M25 motorway

Aldersford Park has become a country club, Much of the land round the lake has been taken up by a golf course (**6**). In 1978 the fine avenue of elms had to be cut down because the trees were diseased. New trees have been planted (**7**).

Abbey Farm has changed hands several times recently (**8**). Most people say it is too small to make money. Much of the land has been turned over to soft fruit where people can come and pick their own strawberries (**9**). In the green-

house the farmer is growing pot plants but fuel costs are a problem. He also has a unit of pigs. Some of the land is rented out as a garden centre (**10**). This is doing excellent trade and the owner would like to expand.

Across the river a new school (**11**) has been built to replace the old Victorian school house. There are plenty of windows for everyone to look out of, but in summer the classrooms get almost too hot. Fortunately there is a new leisure centre next door (**12**) which has replaced the public baths. Today only a few houses in Aldersford lack a bath.

Each year tens of thousands of people come to look round the ruins of the monastery – so many, in fact, that a car park has been created and lavatories installed (**13**).

What do you think the monks would have made of these twentieth-century visitors? How surprised they would be to learn that the abbot's house has recently been bought by a computer company wishing to use it as their headquarters (**14**).

Tesco superstore in north-west London.

Aldersford Town Trail

Today Aldersford is a rich mixture of the old and the new. As you walk through the town you will see buildings of many different centuries.

On the top of the hill is the keep built by the Normans. If you walk down Castle Street you can admire the fine Georgian houses built against the castle walls.

The market house still obstructs the traffic in the centre of Market Row, and its arches still provide shelter for shoppers and traders.

Cross the road, go through the lychgate and walk through the churchyard. On the other side of the church you will find Aldersford's newest building: the leisure centre.

Notice the massive thick walls of the Keep and the arched windows. The doorway was placed on the first floor making it easier to defend. Later on the Victorians added the battlement.

Some of the Georgian houses in Aldersford hide much older timber-framed buildings of the sort that can be seen around Northgate. Notice the cast iron railings. These houses have sub-basements in which servants used to work.

The old market house is in need of renovation, but how should it be used? Now that the by-pass has been built, some people would like to see this market area turned into a pedestrian precinct. A decorated Victorian pillar box is still in daily use.

Some people in Aldersford were shocked and angered by the modern design of the new Leisure Centre. They felt it didn't fit in with the old Church nearby—what do you think? Nevertheless it has proved to be very popular, especially with young people.

Aldersford Country Trail

Over the centuries Aldersford has gradually spread out over the surrounding countryside close to the town. Very little farming land remains but there is still much of interest to see. A good starting point for a country walk is the old railway station. The railway of course has gone, but the track has been turned into a nature trail.

Another good walk starts at Aldersford Dock and crosses the footbridge over the river. On your right is the cricket ground. On your left Abbot's House where the town's first computer firm has set up business. Beyond the house, the monastery ruins wait to be explored.

The Aldersford Bypass has greatly improved the quality of life in the town. More parking spaces are needed, even though the car stack near Southgate is now open. Some people argue that the more parking spaces are provided, the more cars will be attracted-so the town will be no better off!

Few people can afford to live in houses like this today. The company which runs the Country Club is finding the place expensive to maintain. It wants to build lots of new houses in the park. Do you think this should be allowed?

ALDERSFORD HOUSE
COUNTRY CLUB

At least the future of the old windmill is safe. A retired business man has carefully restored it to working order. However, he is not interested in opening the mill to the public. Everybody enjoys watching the sails go round, but some people feel the owner shouldn't just keep the mill to himself.

The Monastery attracts plenty of visitors each year. People enjoy walking around the masses of grey stone thinking about the people who used to live here.
I wonder what the Monks who built the Monastery, all those years ago, would have made of us?

47

In Newcastle buildings of many different periods cluster round the market place. Which do you think is the oldest? You may like to know that many of the themes which have been introduced in this book are explored further in the BBC Schools Television series *Now and Then*.